ERNIE

Ernie Banks sits on the dugout steps before the 1969 opener at Wrigley Field and signs scorecards for fans. (Phil Mascione, Chicago Tribune)

AUG 2017

Chicago Tribune

Passing an image of Ernie Banks on the ballpark's façade, fans sprint up the ramp to Wrigley Field's upper deck before a game on May 2, 2013. (Phil Velasquez, Chicago Tribune)

This book is book is available in quantity at special discounts for your group or organization. For further information, contact:

Triumph Books LLC
814 North Franklin Street
Chicago, Illinois 60610
Phone: (312) 337-0747
www.triumphbooks.com

Printed in U.S.A.
ISBN: 978-1-62937-170-2

Content packaged by Mojo Media, Inc.
Joe Funk: Editor
Jason Hinman: Creative Director

This book was created by the staff of the *Chicago Tribune* using material from the newspaper's archives.

All cover photos courtesy of the *Chicago Tribune.*

Editor's note: Due to newspaper practices of the time, you will see some hand-painted edges and other marks from newspaper retouchers, who insured that photographs would print on the presses correctly for newsprint.

Contents

The greatest Cub 6

A man for all seasons 22

Ernie Banks career milestones 28

Where it all began 34

Let's win two – Banks first in NL
to win back-to-back MVP awards 40

Elite – even among his peers 46

One amazin' summer 52

Ernie gave the city a reason
to smile during volatile '60s 64

Banks hits No. 500, joins exclusive club 70

Twilight time: In final season of historic
career, Banks stays positive to the end 78

Ernie reflects upon entering Hall of Fame 84

Banks goes to bat for Cubs, even on first tee 90

Playing game of life – and winning 96

If racial bias hurt, he never showed it 102

Behind the sunny disposition,
a competitive fire burned 112

Always sunny 118

So long, Mr. Cub 122

Ernie by the numbers 126

1931-2015

The greatest Cub

Originally published January 25, 2015

By Paul Sullivan

Ernie Banks passed away Jan. 23, 2015, at the age of 83, but his DNA will be embedded forever in the game of baseball. Aside from his 512 home runs, back-to-back Most Valuable Player awards and first-ballot induction into the Hall of Fame, the Cubs' first black player put the "friendly" into the "Friendly Confines" of Wrigley Field and became synonymous with sunshine.

No, Mr. Cub wasn't the last of a breed. He was a true original, a once-in-a-lifetime athlete whose vibrant personality was part of the package, spreading the gospel of Cubs' baseball to the masses long after his playing days had ended.

Nothing could ruin Ernie Banks' positive vibes, not even the luckless team he made you love.

"Ironically, the guy with the sunniest disposition was really the face of their franchise," former Cubs' executive and current Blackhawks President John McDonough said. "You could argue he was the greatest baseball player in the history of Chicago, but he would never talk about his own career."

Banks' numbers spoke loud enough. A 14-time All-Star, he became the ninth player to reach the 500-home run plateau in 1971, only to be passed by a number of Steroid Era suspects, among others, knocking him down to 22nd place.

No matter. Anyone who spent a moment in Banks' company quickly discovered he was more than just a ballplayer, and his numbers never could define him.

"You didn't have to be around baseball to understand what a great person he was," former Cubs manager Dusty Baker said.

"I know he was Mr. Cub, but he really was Mr. Baseball," White Sox Chairman Jerry Reinsdorf said. "He was really a great, great ambassador for the game."

Though baseball made him a celebrity, Banks was always curious and up for new challenges. In 1963, he unsuccessfully ran for 8th Ward alderman as a Republican in Chicago.

In the summer of '69, he was appointed to the board of the CTA, which led to speculation in the Tribune that he was planning to retire, "especially if the Cubs win the pennant and the World Series." (Spoiler alert: They did not.)

Banks once owned his own sports marketing firm, "Ernie Banks International," was employed by New World Van Lines moving company and

Ernie Banks was the first National League player to win consecutive Most Valuable Player awards, earning the honors in 1958 and 1959. (John Austad, Chicago Tribune)

even dabbled in the media, writing a column in the Tribune and serving as a part-time sportscaster on WGN-9 news. Banks often would be seen narrating his own highlights, famously saying: "And then, I came to the plate ..."

Banks was divorced three times before marrying Liz Ellzey, who survives him, in 1997. His previous wives were Molly Ector (1953-59), Eloyce Johnson (1959-82) and Marjorie Banks (1984-97). He had three children with Johnson — Joey, Jan and Jerry — and a daughter, Alyna Olivia, with Ellzey.

Aside from his home run prowess, the perennial optimist also was renowned for his annual slogans, assuring Cubs fans their high hopes ultimately would be rewarded.

"The Cubs will come alive in '65," Banks proclaimed before the team ended with 90 losses and an eighth place finish.

"The Cubs will shoot from the hip with 'Leo the Lip,'" he announced when new manager Leo Durocher came on board in 1966. The Cubs finished in 10th, tying a franchise record with 103 losses.

Undeterred, Banks predicted the following spring "the Cubs will be heavenly in '67." The awkward rhyme worked, relatively speaking. The Cubs won 84 games and finished in third in '67, and actually spent some time in first place during the summer.

The resurgence of the late '60s led to Banks' most memorable slogan: "The Cubs will shine in '69." They did indeed shine until September, when a late-season collapse spoiled an otherwise glorious summer, adding to their litany of futility.

Nearly five decades later, in spite of the nightmarish ending, that '69 team led by Banks, Ron Santo, Billy Williams and Fergie Jenkins remains the most beloved in Cubs' history.

Ernie Banks makes his final Cubs convention appearance in January of 2014. (Nancy Stone, Chicago Tribune)

"When I started to play baseball, I just had the natural, quick hands. That was my extra advantage, my slight edge over anybody else. ... I could wait until the last minute and hit the ball." –Ernie Banks

The second of 12 children, Banks was born in a poor household in Dallas on Jan. 31, 1931. He grew up picking cotton while playing softball, football and baseball at Booker T. Washington High School, and told sportswriter Phil Rogers in the biography "Ernie Banks" that picking cotton and stuffing it in a sack taught him how to use his hands.

"When I started to play baseball, I just had the natural, quick hands," Banks said. "That was my extra advantage, my slight edge over anybody else. ... I could wait until the last minute and hit the ball."

Banks' patented stance, and that hypnotic wriggling of his fingers on the handle of his bat, one day would be emulated by legions of kids. Those quick hands made Banks stand out among his peers, and at the age of 17, with the help of former Negro leagues pitcher Bill Blair, he became part of a touring team based in Amarillo, Texas.

By 1950 Banks was playing professionally, albeit for $300 per month, for the Kansas City Monarchs, a Negro League team managed by Buck O'Neil. After a couple of years in the Army, he returned to the Monarchs in 1953 and began making a name for himself.

Banks might have wound up with the White Sox, if not for a rare bad defensive game in a Negro Leagues All-Star Game at old Comiskey Park. Legendary scout Hugh Alexander, then working for the Sox under general manager Frank Lane, told sportswriter Jerome Holtzman he was the first one to truly scout Banks, traveling through Colorado, South Dakota and Kansas to see the skinny, athletic shortstop.

"When I got through looking at him, Lane said 'What do you think?'" Alexander recalled in "The Jerome Holtzman Baseball Reader." "I said, 'I'm not sure he can play shortstop, but he can hit with power.' Lane decided he'd take a look for himself. ... After the All-Star Game, Frank told me, 'I don't like Banks as a ballplayer.' I said, 'By God, I do. Why don't you like him?' (Lane said) 'He made two errors in the All-Star Game.'

"I told him, 'Frank, don't pay attention to that. He can hit. Anyway, he'll make a good third baseman.'"

Alexander said Lane told him to contact the Monarchs owner and make a low offer. Alexander knew Banks had gotten better offers, so he never contacted the owner.

In '53, the Cubs wanted an African-American roommate for Gene Baker, a promising black player who was on their Triple-A team. The team purchased Banks and Bill Dickey from the Monarchs on Sept. 8, 1953, and Banks made his big league debut on Sept. 17, beating Baker to the club by three days.

Unlike most modern-day sluggers, Ernie Banks had a compact swing and favored a loose grip on the bat. (Edward Feeney, Chicago Tribune)

Banks went 0-for-3 with an error that day in a 16-4 loss to the Phillies before a crowd of 2,793, but cranked his first home run, off a Gerry Staley knuckleball, three days later. Cubs announcer Bert Wilson nicknamed him "Bingo" while naming second baseman Baker "Bango," ensuring a lyrical double play combination with first baseman Steve Bilko — a "Bingo-Bango-Bilko double play."

Banks was an immediate hit, and in 1955 broke the all-time record for home runs by a shortstop in a season, 39, finishing with 44, including five grand slams, another record that stood until 1987. Despite playing for awful Cubs teams, he earned the National League MVP awards in 1958 and '59, and quickly became a household name. He made $27,500 in '58 and got a raise to $45,000 in '59. In

Above: A trio of Cubs Hall of Famers – from left, Ernie Banks, Billy Williams and Ryne Sandberg – take the field during Opening Day festivities at Wrigley Field in 2003. (Phil Velasquez, Chicago Tribune) Opposite: Ernie Banks makes his Hall of Fame acceptance speech on Aug. 8, 1977, in Cooperstown, N.Y. (Walter Kale, Chicago Tribune)

The Cubs infield in 1956: From left, third baseman Don Hoak, shortstop Ernie Banks, second baseman Gene Baker and first baseman Dee Fondy. (Edward Feeney, Chicago Tribune)

his final two seasons, 1970-71, he earned $85,000 in each. (His salary as CTA board member, a post he held from 1969 to 1981, paid $15,000 annually.)

In a concession to age and knee trouble, Banks' shift from shortstop to first base began in '61, when he also spent time in left field, a position he had suggested to the College of Coaches managing the team. But "head coach" Elvin Tappe said Banks complained of being bored with the lack of action in left.

"The Banks of today little resembles the Cub shortstop of yesteryear," Tribune sportswriter Edward Prell wrote. "He has become quiet and evinces signs of despondency and the old bounce has disappeared."

Banks wound up at first the rest of his career, and if he indeed had lost his bounce, he soon rediscovered it with 37 homers and 104 RBIs in '62. By '64, he was the recipient of his own day, and a large crowd came out to honor him on Aug. 15, including 2,000 Little League and Pony League players who lined the field during ceremonies. Announcer Jack Brickhouse served as master of ceremonies, while Mayor Richard J. Daley proclaimed it Ernie Banks Day.

"First, I want to thank God for making me an American and giving me the ability to become a major league baseball player," Banks said, before thanking his family and the Cubs.

After the '69 collapse, Banks' career was clearly on the wane, but he wanted to go out with at least one World Series. It never happened. The '70 team contended, but by that point his arthritic knees began to affect him, and Banks was limited to 72 games, hitting only 12 homers.

Banks' relationship with Durocher was almost nonexistent by then, and he told friends near the end of the '70 season he would consider retirement

Jalen Johnson, 9, of Chicago, gets some batting tips from Ernie Banks at Wrigley Field in 2005. (Chuck Berman, Chicago Tribune)

rather than endure the "humiliation" of sitting on the bench in 1971.

But Banks returned for '71, appearing in only 39 games in a season when the clubhouse turmoil grew and players openly rebelled against Durocher. The most prominent "dissidents," according to the Tribune, were Santo, Joe Pepitone, Ken Holtzman and Milt Pappas, though writer Cooper Rollow also pointed out "it is no secret that Banks and Durocher do not like each other."

In September 1971, Cubs owner Philip K. Wrigley took out an ad in the Chicago Daily News to announce Durocher would remain as manager, writing an open letter that said "the 'Dump Durocher Clique' might as well give in." Wrigley signed off by saying "if some of the players do not like it and lie down on the job, during the offseason we will see what we can do to find them happier homes. P.S. If only we could find more team players like Ernie Banks."

"It's a good ad and it's appropriate at this time," Banks remarked, adding he was flattered by the mention. Still, Banks had to be diplomatic. His teammates felt they also were "team players" and Banks didn't need anyone resenting him.

Banks played his final game on Sept. 26 at Wrigley, finishing his career with 512 home runs and 2,583 hits. He missed the final series of the season for personal issues, then sent a letter to his teammates afterward saying he regretted not getting a chance to say goodbye.

That ignited speculation Banks was going to replace Durocher as Cubs' manager. But in November the Cubs announced Banks was stepping down as an active player to become first base coach, not manager.

Ernie Banks flashes a victory sign in front of Wrigley Field on Jan. 19, 1977, after he was elected to the Baseball Hall of Fame in his first year of eligibility. (Ray Gora, Chicago Tribune)

"Managing is a dirty job, it doesn't last long and it certainly isn't anything I'd wish on Banks, who is headed for baseball's Hall of Fame," Wrigley said.

Notified of the announcement while in Arizona, Banks said it was news to him and he hadn't made up his mind about retiring. But his playing career was indeed over, and after a brief time as a coach he began new adventures, including his role as an unofficial baseball ambassador.

Banks became a fixture at the Cubs Conventions, and in 2008 the team finally erected a statue of him outside Wrigley.

"I don't think he missed one Cubs Convention," McDonough said. "He loved being back and being involved. And he was really happy about that statue. It meant a lot to him."

On Nov. 20, 2013, President Barack Obama presented him with the Presidential Medal of Freedom, the nation's highest civilian honor.

Banks' exuberance was his calling card from early on, and his catchphrase line, "Let's play two" was engraved on that statue. His friendly demeanor may be why news of Banks' death touched so many people, leading to heartfelt tributes from countless admirers, including Obama.

He loved being Ernie Banks, and everyone loved Mr. Cub back.

Many years ago, Banks told Holtzman he wanted to be cremated after his death "and have my ashes spread out over Wrigley Field — with the wind blowing out."

There could be no more appropriate tribute to the man who sold day baseball at Wrigley Field to a couple of generations of fans.

Doing it between games of a double-header would be even better. ■

Students at Faulkner Elementary School on Chicago's South Side get some batting tips from Ernie Banks in April of 1969. (Chicago Tribune)

A man for all seasons

Originally published January 25, 2015

By David Haugh

With a familiar glint in his eye and trademark grin on his face, Ernie Banks once revealed a recurring dream of standing on a stage in Stockholm accepting the Nobel Peace Prize.

A friend to presidents and a man who once discussed poverty with Nelson Mandela always wanted to be remembered as much more than a baseball player, not just Mr. Cub and the guy who always wanted to play two.

"I've looked at people who have won it, (Desmond) Tutu, Lech Walesa, people who gave of themselves, helped others and made this a better world," Banks told me. "I can imagine myself in Stockholm. I visualize that, being on that stage. That's the legacy I'm searching for."

The legacy Banks leaves honors a hero to millions of Little Leaguers who grew up loving No. 14, the most positive person in every room he entered. Banks hit 512 career home runs for the Cubs from 1953-71 and touched more lives than any statistician could count. The player known for never winning a World Series never met a stranger, never stopped believing.

Indefatigable enthusiasm made Banks everybody's favorite person in town, let alone baseball player. He was uncommonly curious, courteous, considerate and funny. And he will be sorely missed in Chicago and every baseball city Banks graced with his presence and inimitable style.

On the day in 2013 when Banks learned he was receiving the Presidential Medal of Freedom, his "pinnacle" achievement, he humbly recalled being one of 12 children raised poor in Dallas where he bought his first baseball glove for $2.98.

"I look at my life and any of my 11 brothers or sisters could have done this too, so why me?" Banks said.

Asked that day if the presidential honor sated his desire to realize his goal of winning the Nobel Prize, Banks scoffed.

"I said I haven't done that ... yet," he said, breaking into laughter.

Anybody who encountered Banks laughed a lot. He made everybody in his company feel special, as if they shared a unique connection that turned into the kind of memory so many Chicagoans recalled Friday night. In the latter

In 1960, his last year as a full-time shortstop, Ernie Banks won his first and only Gold Glove. (John Austad, Chicago Tribune)

innings of his life, Banks liked to ask people he just met if they were married, with the hopes of setting them up with their future spouse. He could work a room better than the politicians who would line up to shake his hand. He could be relentless in search of a smile.

"I try to go around and find people to get married all the time," Banks once told the Tribune. "I don't like going to more funerals than weddings so I have to find some way to balance out all the funerals I go to."

As Banks aged gracefully, shuttling between homes in Chicago and Marina Del Rey, Calif., he never stopped swinging for the fences in his mind. Instead of gripping and grinning the days away as one of baseball's cheeriest ambassadors, Banks sought ways to use his platform to fight homelessness and hopelessness. He approached Oprah Winfrey for philanthropic advice. He golfed with Warren Buffett. He reached out to Steve Bartman.

He stayed up nights thinking of solutions to urban problems and considered himself a "social entrepreneur." He took as much pride in breaking racial barriers with the Cubs as he did clearing fences at Wrigley Field.

I once asked Banks why a man so happy spent so much time worrying about issues so heavy. He handed me a seven-paragraph personal statement, summed up best by the last three sentences.

"I want to know what sustains you from the inside when all else falls away. I want to know if you can be alone with yourself. And if you truly like the company you keep in empty moments."

Ernie Banks, left, and Cubs teammate Gene Baker open a new shipment of bats on Aug. 6, 1955. Banks hit 44 home runs that year, with a then-record five grand slams. (Chicago Tribune)

"I golfed with half of the U.S. economy at Augusta National! Here's a young kid from Dallas, Texas, from a family of 12, playing golf at a private club with Warren Buffett and Bill Gates. Is this a great country or what?" –Ernie Banks

Has Chicago ever enjoyed a more fascinating athlete for so long? Banks won two most valuable player awards and was a 14-time All-Star as the best Cubs player ever, but that hardly captures all he accomplished as Mr. Cub. Nor did all of Banks' baseball accolades combined make him prouder than what he achieved going from a boy who grew up in Texas picking cotton into a man who died in Chicago symbolizing hope.

The journey always delighted Banks more than the destination, such as the time he recalled teeing off with billionaires Warren Buffett and Bill Gates.

"I golfed with half of the U.S. economy at Augusta National!" Banks said, pumping his fist. "Here's a young kid from Dallas, Texas, from a family of 12, playing golf at a private club with Warren Buffett and Bill Gates. Is this a great country or what?"

It's one a little sadder without Ernie. ■

Right: Ernie Banks – shown here in 1953, his first season with the Cubs – had a slender build but generated home-run power with his wrists and a strong lower body. Opposite: Cubs manager Phil Cavaretta greets Ernie Banks at Wrigley Field on Sept. 14, 1953. Banks, who starred with the Kansas City Monarchs in the Negro Leagues, was the Cubs' first black player. (Edward Feeney, Chicago Tribune)

Ernie Banks career milestones

FIRST GAME

Banks makes his Cubs debut on Sept. 17, 1953, at age 22. He starts at shortstop and bats seventh, becoming the first African-American player in team history. The first pitcher Banks faces is the Phillies' Curt Simmons, who would later be a Cubs teammate. Banks goes 0-for-3 with a walk and a run scored in a 16-4 loss at Wrigley Field.

FIRST HIT

In his second game as a Cub on Sept. 19, 1953, Banks gets his first hit, a single, and goes 2-for-5 with a walk and two RBIs as the Cubs beat the Cardinals 5-2 in St. Louis.

FIRST HOME RUN

On Sept. 20, 1953, in his third game as a Cub, Banks hits his first home run off the Cardinals' Gerry Staley. Banks adds a triple and a single, going 3-for-4 with three RBIs, but the Cubs lose 11-6 in St. Louis.

FIRST WRIGLEY FIELD HOME RUN

On Sept. 26, 1953, in the next-to-last game of the season, Banks homers off Staley again, helping the Cubs to a 4-3 win over the Cardinals at Wrigley.

FIRST OPENING DAY

Banks is the Cubs' starting shortstop on April 13, 1954, and drives in two runs as the Cubs rout the Cardinals 13-4 in St. Louis.

FIRST MULTI-HOMER GAME

On Aug. 22, 1954, Banks homers twice in a 12-6 loss to the Braves at Wrigley Field.

FIRST GRAND SLAM

On May 11, 1955, with Gene Baker, Bob Speake and Elvin Tappe aboard in the bottom of the first inning, Banks homers to left center off Brooklyn's Russ Meyer for his first career grand slam. The Cubs go on to win 10-8. Banks would hit five grand slams that season, setting a single-season record that would stand for more than 30 years.

FIRST FULL SEASON

Banks plays in all 154 games and finishes second in the 1955 National League Rookie of the Year voting behind St. Louis' Wally Moon, but ahead of Milwaukee's Gene Conley (third) and Henry Aaron (fourth).

FIRST ALL-STAR SELECTION

Banks is the starting shortstop for the National League in the 1955 All-Star Game, held in Milwaukee's County Stadium. He goes 0-for-2 in a 6-5 NL victory. Banks would be an NL All-Star 11 times in his 19-year career.

100TH HOME RUN

In the first game of a doubleheader on June 9, 1957, Banks makes a rare start at third base and connects for his 100th career homer, a three-run shot off the Phillies' Robin Roberts. The Cubs win 7-3. Banks would hit 15 of his 512 career homers off Roberts, more than any other pitcher.

Ernie Banks led the league (or tied for the lead) in games played six times in seven seasons from 1954 to 1960. (John Austad, Chicago Tribune)

FIRST MVP AWARD

With his 47 homers, 129 RBIs and .313 average, Banks is voted the NL's most valuable player in 1958, despite the fact that the Cubs finish tied for fifth place, 20 games behind the first-place Braves. Banks wins the MVP award again in 1959, becoming the first back-to-back winner in NL history.

200TH HOME RUN

Banks' 200th is a two-run shot off Milwaukee's Carl Willey on June 14, 1959. The Cubs blank the Braves 6-0 at Wrigley as Dick Drott throws a complete-game shutout, his only victory of the season.

FIRST GOLD GLOVE

Banks wins the National League Gold Glove award at shortstop in 1960. He and Don Kessinger (1969, 1970) are the only Cubs shortstops to win a Gold Glove, which was first awarded in 1957.

FIRST GAME AT FIRST BASE

The Cubs try Banks in left field for a few weeks in 1961, then at first base, where he plays for the first time on June 16. Banks moves back to shortstop in July and stays there through the end of the '61 season. In 1962, he opens the season at first base and stays there almost exclusively through the remainder of his career.

300TH HOME RUN

On April 18, 1962, Banks hits a game-winning solo homer off Houston reliever Turk Farrell in the bottom of the 10th to give the Cubs a 3-2 win at Wrigley.

400TH HOME RUN

With Billy Williams and Ron Santo on base, Banks hits a three-run homer off St. Louis' Curt Simmons in the third inning of a 5-3 Cubs win on Sept. 2, 1965 at Wrigley.

500TH HOME RUN

Banks joins an elite club when he hits his 500th career homer, a solo shot off Atlanta's Pat Jarvis at Wrigley Field on May 12, 1970. The first-place Cubs win 4-3 in 11 innings. At the time, he is just the ninth player to reach the 500 mark.

512TH HOME RUN

The final home run of Banks' career comes at Wrigley on Aug. 24, 1971, when he connects off Cincinnati's Jim McGlothin. Banks' fourth-inning homer ties the game at 3, but the Cubs lose 5-4.

FINAL GAME

On Sept. 26, 1971, at Wrigley, the 40-year-old Banks gets his final hit, an RBI single in the first inning off the Phillies' Ken Reynolds that gives the Cubs a 1-0 lead. It turns out to be the Cubs' only run that day. Banks finishes 1-for-3 with a walk and the Cubs lose 5-1.

HALL OF FAME

In 1977, his first year of eligibility, Banks is inducted into the Baseball Hall of Fame.

PRESIDENTIAL MEDAL OF FREEDOM

On Nov. 20, 2013, President Barack Obama awarded Banks the Presidential Medal of Freedom, one of the highest honors a U.S. civilian can receive.

In 1968, the Cubs finished above .500 for the second straight season, the first time in Ernie Banks' career that the team posted back-to-back winning records. (Phil Mascione, Chicago Tribune)

Always a man of the people, Ernie Banks seemed to enjoy meeting fans as much as they enjoyed meeting him. (Phil Mascione, Chicago Tribune)

Where it all began

Originally published April 11, 2011

By Phil Rogers

On his first morning as a professional baseball player — a semi-pro, really — Ernie Banks awoke in a room at the Mount Olive Hotel in Amarillo, Texas, that he shared with Marvin Hickman, a friend from Dallas who also had been picked for tryouts. They had laughed during the night about a hole in the roof, which allowed them to peer upward and see the night sky. Hickman, Banks remembered, called it the "starlight room."

It was an introduction to the crude conditions of baseball on the game's margins, where both hunger and a healthy appetite could keep players going for decades while traveling in circles. Banks was thrilled to be there and even happier when he was selected as the Colts' starting shortstop.

Pay would be determined by the size of the crowds, but it was usually about $5 per player, sometimes less, sometimes more. It didn't take long for Banks to ease anyone's doubts that a 17-year-old kid could survive in a league filled with hardened men, many in their 30s and some even in their 40s. He hit a home run to left-center on his third at-bat in his first game, breaking up a scoreless tie and earning him an immediate reward.

Bill Blair, the Negro leagues veteran who had taken him to Amarillo, rushed up to Banks in the dugout and told him to "get up in the stands and pass your cap." Banks didn't know the custom, which was quickly explained to him, but he wouldn't have to be told twice after he sheepishly moved through the crowd of about 500 fans, who dropped pennies, nickels, dimes, and an occasional quarter into his cap. He would count it after the game — it totaled more than $6.

"I had never made money so easily and so quickly," Banks wrote in "Mr. Cub," an autobiography published in 1971.

The Colts spent the summer traveling through Texas, New Mexico, Oklahoma, Kansas and Nebraska, playing local teams at every stop.

There were frequent bus breakdowns, after which the team's owner, Johnny Carter, would miraculously produce friends with automobiles. When there were no hotels or restaurants in communities where such services were only for whites, Carter would arrange housing with black families.

Banks returned to the Colts the following summer after his junior year at Washington High.

Ernie Banks and his father, Eddie, enjoy a light moment before a game in April of 1969. (Ray Gora, Chicago Tribune)

The kid hit around .350 and had about 15 chances to pass his hat.

One of his best days came against the Kansas City Stars, a feeder team of the legendary Monarchs, in a game played in Lubbock, Texas. The Stars' player-manager was 45-year-old outfielder James "Cool Papa" Bell, who was probably the first to realize Banks' potential.

Bell was struck as much by Banks' calm demeanor on and off the field as his graceful power.

"His conduct was almost as outstanding as his ability," Bell said.

Bell told Banks that he would get an offer from the Monarchs when he had finished high school and would say later that he called first-year manager Buck O'Neil to recommend Banks for a starting position with the Negro American League team. O'Neil, Bell would say, told him that he was happy with his shortstop, Gene Baker.

"Baker was good enough to play several years in the bigs," Bell said, "but he was never Banks' equal."

Somebody was listening to Cool Papa, however.

Banks captained the football team, lettered in basketball and thrilled his mother by completing his courses. The day after graduation, he was on a Greyhound bus bound for baseball's big stage.

The Monarchs, managed by O'Neil, played in the Negro American League's West Division against the Chicago American Giants, the Memphis Red Sox, the Birmingham Black Barons and the Houston Eagles.

"It was a new beginning in my life," Banks said. "I was really traveling. I was meeting people from all over. I was seeing other cities. My eyes were opened." ∎

Excerpted from 'Ernie Banks: Mr. Cub and the Summer of '69,' by Phil Rogers, Triumph, 233 pages, $24.95

Above: Despite an MVP season from Ernie Banks, the 1958 Cubs finished tied for fifth place, 20 games behind first-place Milwaukee in the National League. Opposite: Ernie Banks looks through his fan mail on July 7, 1955. Banks' performance and outgoing personality made him an instant hit with the Cubs' faithful. (Chicago Tribune)

Autograph seekers reach out to Ernie Banks before a game at Wrigley Field in 1971. (Phil Mascione, Chicago Tribune)

Let's win two – Banks first in NL to win back-to-back MVP awards

Originally published November 5, 1959

By Edward Prell

Ernie Banks, the Chicago Cubs' 28-year-old slugging shortstop, set a precedent Wednesday when he was named the National League's most valuable player for the second successive year.

Never before had this high honor been won in consecutive seasons in the National League. Banks became the fourth National Leaguer to win the award more than once. Roy Campanella and Stan Musial were three-time winners. Carl Hubbell, pitching star two decades ago for the New York Giants, twice was selected.

Eddie Mathews of the Milwaukee Braves was runner-up to Banks and third place went to Hank Aaron, the Braves' National League batting champion of 1959.

Banks was elected by a committee of baseball writers from the eight National League cities. Votes of two of the 24 members were thrown out when their ballots were late reaching the office of Hy Hurwitz, secretary-treasurer of the Baseball Writers Association of America.

Banks polled 232½ votes, Mathews 189½, and Aaron 174. Wally Moon, Los Angeles outfielder, was fourth with 161. They were followed by Sam Jones and Willie Mays of the Giants and Roy Face, Pittsburgh relief pitcher.

The Cubs' slugger, whose performance generally was credited with keeping his team out of the cellar, or at least seventh place, had 10 of the 22 votes for first place and tied for the top spot with Mathews on another ballot. Mathews drew five first-place votes, Aaron two, and Moon one.

The Cub star's clear-cut superiority could not be denied despite the fact that players on second-division clubs seldom are selected. The Cubs finished fifth last season and tied for the same position in 1958.

Banks came into his own last season as a defensive shortstop, making only 12 errors to set a new major-league record for the position. He led the majors in runs batted in [143] but was beaten out for the majors' home-run crown when Mathews hit his 46th homer in the second game of the

One of Ernie Banks' trademark slogans was "Let's play two." (William Yates, Chicago Tribune)

> "So many players in our league had great, great years that I hadn't thought much about getting the award again. It makes me feel real good."
> –Ernie Banks

Braves' title playoff with the Los Angeles Dodgers.

Mathews batted in 114 runs and hit .306. Aaron hit .355 to win the batting title while hitting 39 homers and driving in 123 runs. Ernie's batting average was .304, tenth best in the NL.

Banks won MVP honors last year with 283 of a possible 1,416 points. Following Ernie in the 1958 balloting were Mays and Aaron. In 1958, Banks hit 47 homers and drove in 129 runs — both major-league highs — and batted .313 with a slugging percentage of .616.

"Are you kidding? That's wonderful," exclaimed Banks when the Tribune told him he was Mr. Big once again in 1959. "I certainly didn't expect it. So many players in our league had great, great years that I hadn't thought much about getting the award again. It makes me feel real good."

Banks, recently remarried, was in the process of moving into a new house on Chicago's South Side. He said he has made only one banquet appearance since the season ended. He plans to resume his disc-jockey program soon. In the meantime, Ernie has been signing baseballs and giving tips to youngsters each Saturday under sponsorship of a South Side automobile dealership. ■

As the Braves' Henry Aaron looks on, Ernie Banks points his bat toward his favorite Wrigley Field home run target in 1957. Banks finished with 43 homers that year, second only to Aaron's 44 in the National League. (Chicago Tribune)

Ernie Banks hoists a fan's homemade sign before the Cubs played the Cardinals on Aug. 15, 1968, at Wrigley Field. (Edward Feeney, Chicago Tribune)

Elite – even among his peers

Originally published January 25, 2015

By Mark Gonzales

Jim Marshall remembers the shortest scouting meeting Giants manager Alvin Dark ever had before a three-game series at Wrigley Field in 1961.

"Just walk Ernie Banks four times and we'll win this series," Marshall recalled.

Marshall and several former Cubs shared the admiration and respect they possessed for Banks after a storied 19-year playing career — in a special era that included fellow Hall of Famers Willie Mays, Mickey Mantle and Henry Aaron.

"Ernie was one of the best ambassadors baseball has ever seen," Aaron said in a statement. "He was a dear friend of mine, and I will miss him and his honesty."

And as far as Jerry Kindall is concerned, Banks more than held his own with those Hall of Fame players despite never advancing to the postseason.

"I was blessed to have played in that era," said Kindall, who was with the Cubs for at least parts of five seasons (1956-58, '60-61) during a 10-year career as an infielder.

"Ernie was one of the greatest hitters of his time."

Although Banks hit fewer home runs (512) than Aaron, Mays and Mantle and drove in fewer runs (1,636) than Aaron and Mays, he earned just as many National League most valuable player awards (1958-59) as Mays and was a 14-time All-Star despite switching from shortstop to first base midway through his career.

"His home runs were a picture to watch," Kindall said. "They were rising line drives. Many of them were hit into a strong jet stream."

Cubs historian Ed Hartig wrote in an email: "The numbers only tell a small part of the story. He put up those numbers as the first African-American player in franchise history, playing in a day when he often couldn't eat in the same restaurant as the rest of the team or stay at the same hotel. Yet Ernie more than survived, he thrived."

As a youngster with the Braves, Dusty Baker was mentored by Aaron and immediately recognized the camaraderie that Banks possessed with teammates and fellow Hall of Famers Billy Williams, Ferguson Jenkins and Ron Santo.

"He schooled Billy Williams when Billy came up from the minors, and Billy is one of my favorites," said Baker, who went on to manage the Cubs from 2003-06. "He showed a genuine interest in you as a player and as a person."

Ernie Banks receives his 1959 National League Most Valuable Player award from league president Warren Giles prior to a game at Wrigley Field in May of 1960. (Chicago Tribune)

Banks also never displayed a sense of entitlement, regardless of his stature.

In 1956, Cubs pitchers Don Kaiser and Moe Drabowsky and Kindall were "bonus babies," which meant they must stay in the majors for two calendar years because of their sizable bonuses. That caused tension among their teammates, who felt they hadn't "proven their way" to the majors, Kindall recalled.

"But we were no different in Ernie's mind," Kindall said. "He was Mr. Cub treating us like normal Cubs players, trying to help us win."

Marshall, 83, a special adviser with the Diamondbacks, recalled the courage Banks displayed while in the midst of a tense series with the Giants in 1959 that resulted in Banks getting drilled in the lower back and eventually leaving the game.

"I'm thinking there's no way he'll play the next day," said Marshall, who played with Banks in 1958-59 and managed the Cubs from 1974-76 after Banks had retired. "He couldn't walk up the stairs to the clubhouse.

"He didn't work out before the next game and barely made it out to shortstop. And then he hits a home run in the first inning."

Kindall, 79, thanked Banks for being so good at shortstop he caused Kindall to move to second base and extend his career with the Indians and Twins.

"Ernie had a great pair of hands," said Kindall, who won three NCAA titles in 24 seasons as head coach at Arizona. "He wasn't flashy and didn't have a strong arm, but he always found the right grip to make a strong throw." ■

Ernie Banks gives his oldest daughter Jan a kiss on May 13, 1969. Jan and her schoolmates from Faulkner Elementary School were Banks' guests at Wrigley Field. (Ray Gora, Chicago Tribune)

Ernie Banks, center, is flanked by (from left) catchers Dick Bertell and Merritt Ranew, head coach Bob Kennedy and pitcher Dick Ellsworth before the home opener in 1964. (Tom Kinahan, Chicago Tribune)

One amazin' summer

Originally published June 11, 1989

By Fred Mitchell

The legend, the lingering mystique of the 1969 Cubs seems disingenuous. To build a shrine of memories to immortalize a second-place ballclub seems to contradict our sporting nation's preoccupation with worshipping champions.

But to Chicago sports fans of a certain age, that Cubs team will never be forgotten. Decades after that cruel and unforgiving season, fans find themselves replaying those final weeks when the Amazin' Mets, a 100-to-1 shot to win it all, overtook the Cubs en route to an improbable World Series triumph over the Baltimore Orioles.

"Usually, when you finish second, nobody remembers," Hall-of-Fame outfielder Billy Williams said. "But the situation was a little different for the '69 club because we had played together so long. A lot of people in Chicago and a lot of people around the country knew about the '69 Cubs."

"Because we didn't win the pennant doesn't make us bad guys," Cubs catcher Randy Hundley said. "Baseball guys sometimes say that because you didn't win the pennant, you're a loser. Well, I've got news for you: I'm not a loser.

"We gave it all we had. One thing I'm comfortable with 20 years later is that we gave everything we had. If you stop to think, where we would be if we had won the pennant? Who knows? We may not have the friendships on the team that we do today. Those things last a lifetime."

Ron Santo, the hard-hitting Gold Glove third baseman who used to leap off the ground and click his heels in exultation after each victory, was constantly reminded of that season up until his death in 2010.

"I saw that movie 'Field of Dreams' and I could really relate to that scene where those ballplayers get together in that Iowa cornfield and play a game," Santo said. "It really touched me. That's how I feel sometimes. I wish we could play over some of those games against the Mets."

From pinch-hitter Willie Smith's dramatic game-winning home run in the bottom of the 11th inning on Opening Day against the Phillies, the Cubs, who had endured 20 consecutive second-division finishes (from 1947 to '66), appeared destined for their first pennant since 1945.

Managed by Leo "the Lip" Durocher, the Cubs led the Mets by 9½ games on Aug. 14. They led by 5 with 25 games to go. But the Mets, behind superb

Behind Ernie Banks' smile and sunny disposition was a competitive fire that helped make him one of the game's greatest players. (Chicago Tribune)

Most games played without reaching the postseason

Player	Years played	Seasons	Games
Ernie Banks	1953-71	19	2,528
Luke Appling	1930-50	20	2,422
Mickey Vernon	1939-60	20	2,409
Buddy Bell	1972-89	18	2,405
Ron Santo	1960-74	15	2,243

Source: Baseball-reference.com

pitching, won 38 of their final 49 games. After Sept. 5, the Cubs were listed in critical condition, losing seven straight, 10 of 11 and 14 of their last 20. They were eliminated on Sept. 24.

Although every baseball fan had already heard of Ernie Banks, the names of Santo, Williams, Hundley, Glenn Beckert, Don Kessinger, Ferguson Jenkins, Jim Hickman and Ken Holtzman were gaining prominence.

Banks, Mr. Cub, wound up his 17-year Hall of Fame career with 512 home runs and two MVP awards, but no championships. In 1969, at the age of 38 and with wobbly knees, Banks cranked out 23 home runs and 106 RBIs while playing first base.

"I would say there were at least 11 of us who were together nine years, and you don't find that very often," said Santo, who hit .289 with 29 homers and 123 RBIs in 1969. "And Billy, Ernie and I played for 14 years together. We got very close."

Time failed to heal the wounds the Mets inflicted on Santo.

Santo was the only former Cub who refused to play in a "Dream Game" exhibition against the 1969 Mets that was staged in the mid-'80s in Phoenix.

"I don't care what they would pay, I would not play. That was too much hurt," Santo said. "I don't

At age 38, Ernie Banks, shown here on his way to home plate after a home run, hit 23 homers and drove in 106 runs for the 1969 Cubs. (Chicago Tribune)

take anything away from them. The Mets had a great pitching staff. I still, to this day, don't feel they have the ballclub that we had.

"However, they won and they beat the Orioles in the World Series. But they rubbed it in. I'll never forget that. It wasn't just that they beat us. They rubbed our face in it.

"There are a lot of good guys on that ballclub and I don't have anything personal against anybody. But it's just the Mets, period. It wouldn't be any fun for me to go to a 'Dream Game' against the Mets."

"Maybe the Mets rubbed it in to us," Hundley said, "but if it were reversed, would we rub it in to them? Probably, I think they do it in fun. They are a good bunch of guys.

"Not enough people give the Mets credit for what they did. Who would have predicted they would go on and beat Atlanta (in the National League playoffs) and then the Orioles in the World Series?"

Hundley was involved in a controversial play in New York's Shea Stadium when Tommie Agee was called safe at home plate by umpire Satch Davidson.

Was he out or safe?

"There's no question about it, he was out," Hundley said 20 years later. "He (Agee) finally admitted that I tagged him out. I put the tag on him so hard that I almost dropped the ball."

Fan interest in the Cubs reached new heights in 1969, not to be rivaled again until the club won the NL East in 1984.

With his famous loose-fingered grip, Ernie Banks hit 512 home runs, the second-highest total in Cubs history behind only Sammy Sosa. (Chicago Tribune) Opposite: Ernie Banks sits on the dugout steps before the 1969 opener at Wrigley Field and signs scorecards for fans. (Phil Mascione, Chicago Tribune)

"I only clicked my heels because the fans loved it," said Santo. "We had people traveling with us everywhere. We were like rock stars with fans tearing our shirts off."

With pitcher Dick Selma exhorting the Bleacher Bums by waving a towel and some 20,000 fans arriving early enough at Wrigley Field to watch batting practice, the frolic and anticipation appeared warranted.

"I remember Bill Hands and I went to dinner in St. Louis at Stan Musial's restaurant and we got a standing ovation when we walked to a table," Hundley said. "It was embarrassing as all get-out. But that was an awful lot of fun."

The Cubs' failure to reach the playoffs or World Series in '69 may have delayed Santo's and Jenkins' entry to the Hall of Fame, though they both would be inducted eventually, Santo posthumously. Santo had a .277 career batting average and 342 home runs while playing in 2,243 games. Jenkins, a sturdy right-hander, had a 284-226 record that included six straight seasons of 20 wins or more and 267 complete games.

"I feel Billy (Williams) should have been in the Hall of Fame a lot earlier than he was. But unfortunately, that (postseason play) is what everybody is talking about," Santo said. "Statistic-wise, there are only nine third basemen in the Hall of Fame. And statistic-wise, I'm as good or better. But that doesn't get you there, I guess. I feel that if we had won in '69, we would have won in '70. It would have been the momentum thing, because we were still young."

Ernie Banks hits the second of his two home runs in the Cubs' 1969 opener at Wrigley Field. The Cubs would go on to win 7-6 in 11 innings on Willie Smith's pinch-hit homer. (Ray Gora, Chicago Tribune)

"It was a love-hate relationship I had with Durocher. I loved him one day and hated him the next. As a catcher, he was real tough to play for." –Randy Hundley

Said Williams: "You think of Reggie Jackson and Lou Brock and all the things they were able to do in the World Series. I always wonder what kind of player I could have been in the World Series. I always have that in the back of my mind.

"The fondest memory of the 1969 season for me had to be about midway through the year, June 29, when the Cubs set aside a day for me here at Wrigley Field. Along with the special day, a lot was at stake and we were playing the Cardinals in a double-header. It made it a fantastic day because we beat the Cardinals twice."

The '69 Cubs were led by the irascible yet inspirational Durocher.

"There was no doubt that when Leo came here, in 1966, all of us were awed," Santo said. "I mean, Leo Durocher is going to be our manager! I think it had a lot of effect on turning us around because the other teams knew we had Durocher on our side and he was a competitor. You know, winning is a habit and losing is a habit. We were in a losing habit before Durocher turned it around. I very much enjoyed playing for Leo. We had our differences, but to me there wasn't a better manager."

Hundley had his share of differences with Durocher as well. Durocher, then 63, constantly second-guessed the pitches Hundley called and irritated him to the point of distraction.

"It was tough to take at times," Hundley said. "He wanted me to be the manager on the field. I kept (anger) bottled up inside. Shucks, I was scared to death of him.

"It was a love-hate relationship I had with Durocher. I loved him one day and hated him the next. As a catcher, he was real tough to play for.

"He made me learn the game. I was just fortunate to survive that first year I played for him. I mean, the pitcher could throw the ball down the middle of the plate and anybody could hit it out of the ballpark, but I was the dumb idiot that called the pitch. It was tough to take at times. He was throwing towels on the field to get my attention, second-guessing pitches."

When did it all fall apart?

Center-fielder Don Young caught more than his share of the blame for the collapse because of a dropped flyball in a crucial series in New York.

"When I got back to the hotel after we lost that game, I got a phone call with a guy sobbing and sniffing on the phone. And it was Fergie, because he had pitched that game," Williams said. "He said, 'Can you come down and talk, Billy?' We talked

Ernie Banks runs into the bullpen to grab a foul pop fly during a game at Wrigley Field in 1969. An underrated defensive player, Banks led all NL first basemen with a .997 fielding percentage in '69. (Chicago Tribune)

about the game and I told him: 'You pitched well. It was just a mistake the kid made in the outfield.'

"Santo had said something that day that got in the paper about Young dropping the ball. Ronnie later retracted that statement, but the kid never did play to his potential.

"But we all started making mistakes because we were under pressure and we had never been there before. We couldn't find anything to get us back in the groove."

Santo cited a West Coast trip late in the season.

"Players or managers will always say, 'I don't read the papers or look at the scoreboard.' That's baloney," Santo said. "We went into the West Coast with an eight-game lead. I recall that we lost our first two ballgames on the West Coast and the Mets won their first two. Every time we would go into the ballpark on the West Coast to take hitting practice, their game was over and the Mets won. It was just more and more pressure.

"Then when we came back home from that road trip, our lead went from eight games to 3½. Back in Chicago, the game that always stands out in my mind is against the Pirates. With two outs in the top of the ninth, we were leading by a run and the wind was blowing in a gale. Willie Stargell fouled off four or five pitches against Phil Regan before hitting one completely out of the ballpark to tie the score. I was standing there at third thinking, 'Well, what's going to happen now?' We went extra innings and they ended up beating us. To me, that was the turning point." ■

Billy Williams, Ron Santo and Ernie Banks, left to right, formed the heart of the Cubs' lineup in the 1960s and early '70s. (Phil Mascione, Chicago Tribune)

Ernie gave the city a reason to smile during volatile '60s

Originally published January 25, 2015

By John Kass

If you're feeling a cold wind blow through a hole in Chicago's heart, you know why: Ernie Banks, "Mr. Cub," is dead at age 83.

The eternal optimist is gone.

"The Cubs are due in '62," he'd say. But that didn't happen. That same year, Banks announced his run for Chicago alderman as a Republican, but the Democratic machine defeated him the next February.

It was fortunate. Cubs karma was safe from politics, and Banks was free to make other predictions, including the one that is perhaps the most beautiful and haunting in Cubs history.

"The Cubs will shine in '69," he said, and they did, for a while, long enough to bind people to that North Side team for generations.

As soon as I heard about Banks' passing Friday night, I thought of summer days in Oak Lawn, in White Sox country, and the baseball fields behind the hospital. Every team had three or four kids, even White Sox fans, trying to bat like Ernie Banks:

The bat held straight, fingertips moving, tapping the wood like a clarinet player, no hitting gloves, just touch, letting the ball come into him and then the wrists snapping and line drive home run power.

Banks was a Hall of Fame ballplayer and a great ambassador for baseball and that North Side team, and those who didn't grow up here will latch onto the stuff everyone is talking about — Ernie's kindness, his signature "Let's play two," and that always-sunny disposition of his.

What seems forgotten in the telling of the Ernie Banks story is that, yes, he was optimistic, and yes, he was a great ambassador for the game, but that's not the only reason we mourn him.

There was something terrible happening in Chicago back then. In the late 1960s, the city had become an angry fist.

Kids needed a smile, but we didn't see a smile anywhere. Instead, there were raised voices and raised hands, and killing and burning and looting and protests. And there was also great anger in absolute silence, adults packing up the car and

Ernie Banks slides into home plate after a wild pitch by the Phillies' Jack Baldschun on June 17, 1964. The run gave the Cubs the lead in the 7th inning of a 9-5 victory. (Chicago Tribune)

driving away, while the kids in the backseats looked at their neighborhoods for the last time.

If you saw what happened to Ferguson, Mo., just months ago, that's nothing compared with what it was here, stretches of the West and South sides of Chicago burning, gangs and cops battling, Chicago firefighters worried about being hit by sniper fire.

There were the riots after the assassination of Martin Luther King Jr. in 1968, blood in our streets and Mayor Richard J. Daley famously ordering the police to shoot to kill arsonists.

And then came the Democratic National Convention and the police clubs in the air and the Yippies and the Days of Rage and Daley babbling and becoming an angry cartoon.

People stayed in their neighborhoods. In an attempt to reduce conflict, Daley didn't fill some of the park district neighborhood pools. And residents who'd fled didn't return to the old neighborhoods in the city if they didn't have to.

The people of the white flight suburbs and African-Americans who'd soon be moving to black flight suburbs weren't thinking about patronizing baseball, not in the late 1960s. At least that's how it seemed to me, to 12-year-old eyes, with Sox Park appearing like a ghost town.

But in 1969, an amazing thing happened on the North Side. The Cubs' Willie Smith hit a home run, and the hapless Cubs won their opener.

Announcer Jack Brickhouse screamed with delight, and the miracle unfolded.

The Cubs took off and became legendary on that famous ride into first place for much of that amazing season. Ron Santo kicked his heels. Randy Hundley banked at Uptown Federal Savings. Ernie's smile was everywhere.

Ernie Banks, left, often rode the CTA train from his South Side home to Wrigley Field during his playing career. (Arthur Walker, Chicago Tribune)

Chicago needed the Cubs to win and they did, and the people cleaved to the team. The Cubs had something we needed. They had good news. And people wanted good news.

It wasn't just the winning. It was the way they won, without much controversy and drama — until the black cat and the surge of the Mets and the ultimate heartbreak.

Early on, for most of the summer, it was good news.

Moms became fans, in the days when moms stayed home raising kids and driving them everywhere. You couldn't enter a store and not see some kind of Cubs promotion. The song "Hey Hey, Holy Mackerel!" was everywhere.

And dads got the tickets. My dad wasn't the only one. We avoided Sox Park back then. We sat in Wrigley.

And folks joined the team emotionally, even from Sox country and elsewhere. I'm sure some Cubs marketing study has finally figured that the angry '60s and the Cubs of '69 made that franchise click.

There are many quotes out there now that Ernie Banks has passed. I've been reading them for hours. But it's not the words — it's how he said them.

There was always something of a gentleman in him, a decency in his manner. He was reassuring, not like some cocky sports hero, but more like a teacher.

It was that kindness that kids could see, a concern, and we could hear it in his voice. There was a steadiness to it.

And we've never forgotten it.

So long, Ernie. ■

Manager Bob Kennedy, left, stands on top of the dugout steps at Wrigley Field with his starting lineup for the 1963 opener. Players, left to right, are center fielder Don Landrum, shortstop Andre Rodgers, left fielder Billy Williams, third baseman Ron Santo, first baseman Ernie Banks, right fielder Lou Brock, second baseman Ken Hubbs, catcher Dick Bertell and pitcher Larry Jackson. (Edward Feeney, Chicago Tribune)

Banks hits No. 500, joins exclusive club

Originally published May 13, 1970

By Richard Dozer

The day dawned ugly.

Rain and severe weather darkened Chicago's morning. Downpours made vast puddles in the streets of the city and suburbs. Certainly there'd be no baseball on this horrid day — much less a home run by Ernie Banks.

Then, as though on command, the clouds broke apart. Wisps of fog slithered away. Sweaty workmen rolled back the canvas, and the game was on. But the Atlanta Braves scored twice in the first inning on one sloppy play at the plate, and Ken Holtzman was behind. And 5,264 fans wondered why they'd come — and it was still an ugly day.

Now Ernie Banks was at the plate in the second inning. The Cubs were hitless, and there was only some of the urging that has greeted Mr. Cub at every turn since it became fact last Saturday that his next home run would be his 500th.

Pat Jarvis went one-and-one on Ernie, then served a fastball chest high and a little bit in. Banks swung, and when Rico Carty, the Braves' left fielder, turned toward the seats, Banks knew he had the coveted home run.

The blast turned the day to sunlight and Banks' teammates to a band of determined young men. The Cubs fell back on another cheap run but drove relentlessly from behind, tied the game in the ninth on Billy Williams' 12th home run, and finally won on three singles in the 11th, 4 to 3.

Thus was written another memorable chapter in Wrigley Field, the stately ballpark rich in history — a field that later this year will stand amid new stadiums, coast to coast, as the National League's only link with the past.

The statistical report on yesterday's ball game shows Banks not only with his 500th homer but also with his 1,600th and 1,601st runs batted in. He knocked in Chicago's second run with a sacrifice fly in the seventh inning.

The report further notes that Holtzman and Jarvis went eight innings apiece and therefore did not figure in the decision despite excellent pitching by each. Holtzman was lifted for a pinch-hitter and Jarvis because he became so tuckered

Ernie Banks kisses his 500th home run ball on May 12, 1970 after the Cubs defeated Atlanta 4-3 in 11 innings. "The riches of the game are in the thrills," Banks said later, "not the money." (Ray Gora, Chicago Tribune)

out he had difficulty walking to the dugout at the end of the eighth.

In the realm of relief, the Cubs had the better of it on this muggy day. Ted Abernathy pitched two scoreless innings allowing only Carty's third single of the day. Phil Regan hurled the 11th, interrupted only by an astute decision to give Hank Aaron an intentional walk when the count reached 3 and 1.

The Braves used a pair of former White Sox hurlers in a vain attempt to hold the line. But Hoyt Wilhelm, who let a knuckleball stray too high to Williams, was victim of the tying homer in the ninth and Bob Priddy suffered the loss on a game-winning hit off Sonny Jackson's glove by Ron Santo with the bases full in the 11th.

This was the Cubs' first decision over Atlanta in five meetings, and it set the stage for the first confrontation with a champion in Wrigley Field this season. The New York Mets play here today, with Bill Hands drawing the Mets' Gary Gentry as his pitching opponent.

But what can happen in the Mets series to shove Banks' great day into the background?

It took Ernie 52 minutes to get to the clubhouse after his day of heroics. Interviewed long on radio and television in WGN's booths upstairs, he later submitted to taped sessions with many others. He clasped hands with fans who followed him upstairs and down. He posed on the field for pictures.

When last seen he was accommodating a cameraman who wanted him to imitate Santo's victory hop which became traditional after Wrigley Field triumphs last year — but has been carefully avoided this year.

Under questioning. Ernie admitted that he had been pressing for the first five or six games

Ernie Banks receives a trophy commemorating his 500 home runs as a Cub. (Chicago Tribune)

this season, knowing full well that the 500 homers were in sight. "It hurt my... timing for a while, but my rhythm seems to be back now," he said.

He disclosed that he was looking for the ball inside when Jarvis served it right there. Did he think it was going out?

"I thought the ball had a real good chance," he replied. "Then when I saw Carty turn and look into the seats, I knew it was in."

Banks, who had struck triples into the left-field corners in the Cubs' two previous games, ran as fast as he could to first base before he stole a glance, heard the crowd and broke into his familiar home run trot.

He doffed his cap as lie crossed the plate and shook hands first with Rick Ferrari, the Andy Frain usher chief who arrived conveniently at the plate with a new supply of baseballs for the umpire. Later, after he'd shaken the hand of every teammate in view, he went out to his first base position, received another ovation, and got a congratulatory handshake from Carty on his way to the Atlanta dugout.

"It was senior citizens' day — a great day," bubbled Ernie.

And indeed it was. Not only did senior citizens get in for a reduced price, Ernie was thinking undoubtedly of himself as a senior citizen and also Wilhelm, who at 46, is the major leagues' oldest ball player.

Long before the electrifying conclusion — when things were ugly — Holtzman fell into the Cub habit of walking the first opponent to face him. This time it was Jackson, and his pass was the fourth in a row to go to a man leading off a game here this week.

Cubs third-base coach Peanuts Lowrey congratulates Ernie Banks on his 500th home run. Banks' milestone homer was hit off Atlanta's Pat Jarvis in the second inning of a 4-3 Cubs victory on May 12, 1970. (Phil Mascione, Chicago Tribune)

Felix Millan singled, but Holtzman handled the big men in the Braves' lineup well enough, getting Aaron and Orlando Cepeda on pop fouls while walking Carty to fill the bases. But a wild pitch let Jackson in and when J. C. Martin threw wildly with the recovery. Millan turned a risky dash to the plate into the second run.

After Banks' homered on a pitch Jarvis said he put "right where I wanted it," the Cubs didn't get another hit until Santo doubled to open the seventh. By this time they were behind, 3 to 1, however, on Clete Boyer's double, an infield out, and Holtzman's third wild pitch of the game.

Santo moved to third after his two-bagger when John Callison grounded to first base, then Banks drove his run-scoring fly sharply to Tony Gonzalez in medium center.

Manager Leo Durocher went to a pair of pinch hitters in the eighth, but Jimmie Hall flied deep to right and Willie Smith looked at a third strike before Don Kessinger's single gave the Cubs a wasted base runner.

After Williams' homer created the tie, the teams sparred through a scoreless 10th. Then Kessinger's third single led off the 11th and Glenn Beckert singled through the middle, sending Kessinger to third. Williams got an intentional walk to fill the bases, and with the infield up tight, Santo hit a hard-bounding ball to Jackson. It glanced off Jackson's foot and caromed into short left. There was no pursuit, and the game was over.

The sun was out, and Banks was king. ■

Wrigley Field fans greet Ernie Banks after his 500th career home run on May 12, 1970. The milestone homer came against Pat Jarvis of the Atlanta Braves. (Phil Mascione, Chicago Tribune)

Twilight time: In final season of historic career, Banks stays positive to the end

Originally published August 29, 1971

By Cooper Rollow

Ernie Banks plays little games with people. Nobody is certain exactly what the object of the games is. Perhaps even Banks is not certain.

He will be setting in the sun on a bench along the left-field line in Wrigley Field watching the visiting team take batting practice. An outfielder in visiting grays strolls by, and Banks says: "I LOVE baseball."

The other guy glances over, somewhat startled, until he realizes it is Mr. Cub addressing him, and then he reacts to that remarkable smile as all people do.

"I love baseball too," says the outfielder.

Sandy Koufax, who once threw baseballs for a living and now talks into a microphone, walks by on his way to the broadcast booth and gives Ernie a firm handshake.

"Hey, there's Mr. Pitcher," says Mr. Cub. "Gonna come out of retirement one of these years and start doing your thing again?"

"Not on your life," grins Koufax. "I haven't even touched a baseball this summer."

A man from the press sits down by Ernie, and the big put-on; the big, friendly put-on; the big, friendly, magnificent, sincere put-on, continues.

"Where you been, in the left-field bleachers yesterday?" Banks asks before the sportswriter can pose a single question.

"Tell me, how do those people out there act? Are they behaving nowadays? What, in your opinion, is their real motivation for getting together out there day after day? What do they talk about? Are they good baseball fans? Are they mostly kids? Mostly from the suburbs? How do they get home from the games — ever hear them say? Do they drive or take the train?"

And that's the way it goes. Question after question, with the roles reversed. Why does Ernie like to interview the press rather than vice-versa? Is he practicing for his WGN radio show over the winter?

Ernie won't say why he likes to do the asking. He will do the answering too if you press him, although none of his answers will shock the world with controversy.

"I think I'm improving as an announcer and an interviewer," Banks ventures. "I interviewed (legendary broadcaster) Mel Allen the other day. He said I did fine but that I should learn to talk TO

Ernie Banks tips his cap to the Wrigley Field fans as he approaches home plate after hitting the 500th home run of his career on May 12, 1970. (Phil Mascione, Chicago Tribune)

people rather than AT them."

How about sports other than baseball? When Banks has a microphone in his hand, would he rather talk to basketball, football, or hockey players?

"I mean I REALLY love this game," retorts Banks.

"So do I, so do I," the fellow says hastily.

"I like pro basketball best," Banks says without a moment's hesitation. "I like the sport and I like the guys who play it.

"They're easier for the people in the deprived areas to identify with, and this is a matter that comes close to my heart. They're always going out and making speeches and signing autographs. They give the kids from the poor families somebody to look up to, a goal that is within reach."

Inevitably, the conversation gets around to Banks and his future. He's a player-coach at present, and his name has been mentioned

Above: Ernie Banks played in only 72 games in 1970, the fewest since his debut season. (Chicago Tribune) Opposite: In his role as a member of the CTA board, Ernie Banks listens as CTA chairman James McDonough (left) announces a fare increase on Sept. 2, 1976. (William Yates, Chicago Tribune)

frequently as a potential manager, perhaps the first black manager in the major leagues.

"No, not me, I don't think, not me. You see, I like what you can do as a coach that you couldn't do as a manager. As a coach I can be close to the players, just one of the fellows.

"As a manager, I'd have to be their boss. The relationship would be different and I don't think I'd like it.

"But I'm not thinking about that kind of thing right now. No, siree, I'm just thinking about that old World Series we're going to be in. Just imagine, the Chicago Cubs in the World Series! That's the way it's going to be, for sure." ■

Above: Even in his later years, Ernie Banks (shown here in 2005 at age 74) retained his youthful energy and enthusiasm for life. (Phil Velasquez, Chicago Tribune)
Right: In addition to being an ambassador for baseball, Ernie Banks once said he dreamed of winning the Nobel Peace Prize. (Michael Budrys, Chicago Tribune)
Opposite: Age didn't diminish Ernie Banks' enthusiasm for the game. Here a 39-year-old Banks frolics at the Friendly Confines after smashing his 500th career home run on May 12, 1970. (Ed Wagner Jr., Chicago Tribune)

Ernie reflects upon entering Hall of Fame

Originally published August 6, 1977

By Richard Dozer

It was a sort of bon voyage gathering for Ernie Banks.

Getting Mr. Cub to sit still in Wrigley Field is tough. He's there nearly every day, but usually it's in the role of Pied Piper — tramping the aisles, being trailed by youngsters, signing autographs, and extolling the wonders of day baseball.

But Friday was a special day for Ernie. He's on his countdown to Cooperstown, where Monday he will be enshrined with five others in the baseball Hall of Fame. The hour is close, and Ernie has butterflies.

"It's hard to express what I feel," he told a cluster of reporters, a couple of whom who saw the first game he played for the Cubs back in 1953 and others who came along only at the twilight of his magnificent career. "You wonder if you've really done enough to deserve all of this.

"One of the amazing things to me is all the young kids who hang around me all the time, boys and girls only about 10 years old. I don't think any of them even saw me play."

"That means you're a legend, Ernie," somebody told him.

"Me? A legend? No. But my life is a legend to me. Can you imagine anyone not liking this kind of life?

"All these wonderful cities baseball takes you to — Philadelphia, New York, Pittsburgh. [Ernie was always a National Leaguer, so he didn't mention Cleveland.]

"Travel is a wonderful thing. Baseball players travel more than Henry Kissinger."

Banks said he is fortunate to be reaching the Hall of Fame as a comparatively young man. "Most people have to wait until late in life to get this honor. Many times they are in poor health. I'm lucky. I feel good."

He talked about the old-time ball parks, and said that these are things he'll be thinking about when he reaches Cooperstown, N.Y., Sunday

"I'll remember Crosley Field in Cincinnati, where Freddie Hutchinson was the manager.

Ernie Banks hit a career-high 47 home runs in 1958, one of four straight seasons in which he topped the 40-homer mark. (Chicago Tribune)

They had an outfield with a terrace in it, and when Yogi Berra played there in the World Series, he said he stood back there so he could run downhill after fly balls.

"I liked the clubhouse there, too. It was outside the park, sort of like a little blockhouse. You walked past all those wonderful fans going into the park like a horse coming out of the paddock onto the track.

"And the Polo Grounds with the clubhouse that seemed like a mile away in center field. That could be a depressing walk if you lost. Think of how Ralph Branca must've felt after Bobby Thomson's home run.

"Forbes Field is gone, too, but that was the scene of some great moments in Pittsburgh. They used to call it the 'house of thrills.'"

Banks even recalled Seals Stadium, the transplanted Giants' first home, alongside a brewery in San Francisco. They moved there from New York in 1958, the first of two consecutive years that Banks was the National League's Most Valuable Player — with a club that tied for fifth in an eight-team league.

"I liked that park, too."

It was there in 1959 that Jack Sanford drilled Banks in the back with a "purpose" pitch and put the Cub star out of action for a few days. It was a first, but not for Sanford.

It was the first — and probably the only — time Banks admitted that he felt a pitcher intentionally threw at him. But Ernie didn't want to dwell on anything like that Friday. It's not his game.

Nostalgia is, however, and somebody asked if he would touch on those things in his acceptance speech Monday on the green outside the Hall of Fame Museum. ▪

Teammates Randy Hundley (9), Ron Santo (10) and Billy Williams (26) greet Ernie Banks at home plate after his first-inning home run on April 14, 1968. The Cubs held on to edge the Cardinals 7-6. (Chicago Tribune)

Where Banks hit his 512 home runs

Ballpark	Location	HR
Wrigley Field	Chicago	290
Shibe Park (a)	Philadelphia	39
Sportsman's Park	St. Louis	30
Crosley Field	Cincinnati	27
County Stadium	Milwaukee	24
Forbes Field	Pittsburgh	22
Coliseum	Los Angeles	13
Candlestick Park	San Francisco	12
Ebbets Field	New York	10
Dodger Stadium	Los Angeles	9
Polo Grounds	New York	8
Seals Stadium	San Francisco	7
Fulton County Stadium	Atlanta	6
Shea Stadium	New York	4
Astrodome	Houston	3
Colt Stadium	Houston	3
Busch Stadium	St. Louis	2
Roosevelt Stadium	Jersey City, N.J. (d)	1
Riverfront Stadium (b)	Cincinnati	1
San Diego Stadium (c)	San Diego	1

Source: Baseball-reference.com

(a) Later known as Connie Mack Stadium.
(b) Later known as Cinergy Field.
(c) Later known as Qualcomm Stadium.
(d) Roosevelt Stadium was home to the Brooklyn
     Dodgers for a series of games in 1956 and 1957.

Ernie Banks saves a wild throw from getting into the outfield as the Reds' Johnny Temple steals second in a 1958 game. (Chicago Tribune)

Banks goes to bat for Cubs, even on first tee

Originally published January 10, 1985

By Bob Verdi

Sunshine bathed the Coachella Valley, and Ernie Banks gushed as he dug in at the practice tee.

"God's light, the only kind you need," extolled Banks on a sunny Palm Springs day in January of 1985. "I can't believe what they're talking about doing to Wrigley Field. Night games!! It pains me to think about it. Tradition is nice, but I guess it can't last. Night games in Wrigley Field!! Nooo."

Mr. Cub was making his first appearance in the Bob Hope Classic, a 90-hole melange of pro golfers and celebrities that is the season's first stop on the PGA tour schedule. Banks, an 8-handicapper, was full of his favorite topic, which is life.

"Let's play 18, Ernie," chirped Lee Trevino. "Your Cubs cost me a bundle against San Diego (in the 1984 playoffs). Course, that doesn't bother you. If I had your money, I'd burn mine."

"A 3-0 lead with Rick Sutcliffe on the mound," sighed Ernie. "So close and yet so far. Now they're talking about lights in beautiful Wrigley Field."

"No wonder you love that place," piped up ex-Cincinnati catcher Johnny Bench, swinging a 5-iron like a bat. "The wind's always blowing out. If I played there all my life, I could have hit 500 home runs, too."

"Most beautiful ballpark in the whole world," Banks announced. "Unique. I hope the Cubbies never leave there."

Banks has his address, not his disposition. He works for New World Van Lines in Los Angeles, but plans trips to the company's Chicago headquarters around Cub homestands. Ask him whether he's bitter about being dropped from the team's payroll, and he tells you how marvelous it was to throw out the first ball at October's first playoff game. The only things Mr. Cub rips are his drives, straight down the middle.

"I don't know where I could fit in with the organization," Banks said. "I had a long talk with Dallas Green. But they're still my whole life. I just got cable TV in my home. I can get Channel 9. And now, Lou Brock, a scared kid when he first came up, made it to the Hall of Fame. I was his first

Ernie Banks tips his signature "Mr. Cub" hat during a collectors' convention in Rosemont in 1998. (Heather Stone, Chicago Tribune)

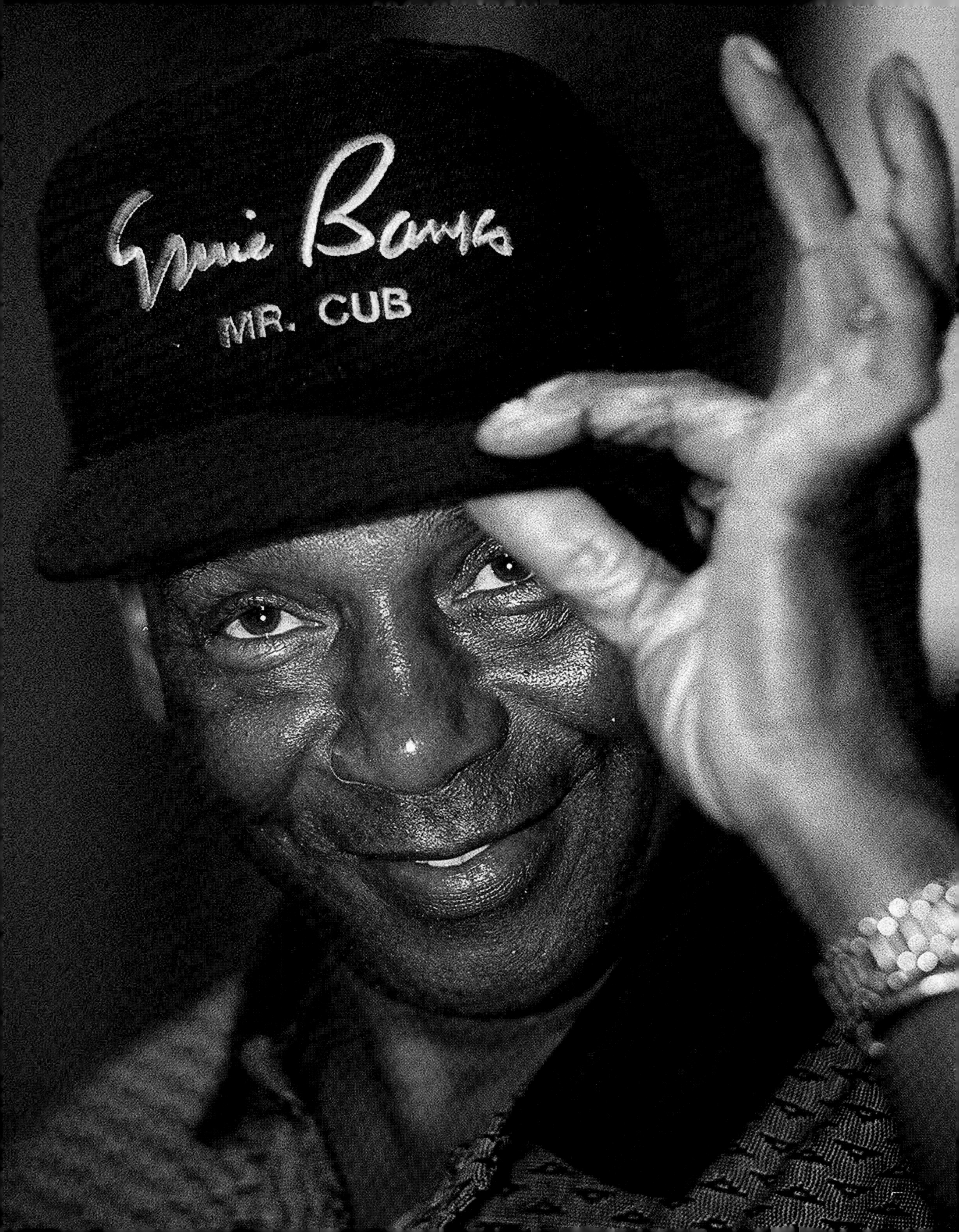
MR. CUB

roommate with the Cubs."

On and on Banks goes, full of hiss and vinegar. If there's a bleak side to his existence, he covers it well. If he ever wakes up on the wrong side of the bed, he keeps it a secret.

"I was in Hawaii and a guy from Alaska comes up to me," Banks said. "He says he gets Channel 9, too. He loves the Cubs. Sunshine and ivy and Wrigley Field. A slice of America."

Even a mention of Leo Durocher escapes Banks' dartboard. During the late '60s, grumpy Leo the Lip failed to worship at Ernie's shrine, often chiding Banks' stature as Mr. Cub. It was impolite, to say the least, but Banks is all blue skies. He's the kind of guy who'd tell you that the nice part about a nuclear war is that it would kill all the mosquitoes, too.

"Leo wasn't jealous of me," Ernie said. "I think he was just trying to push me. You know, when you're in the latter stages of a career like I was, sometimes you get lackadaisical. I understood what he was trying to do. He wasn't trying to embarrass me. There's Ray Floyd!! There's a Cub fan!!"

Cubs, Cubs, Cubs. Cubs in January, Cubs forever with Ernie, even after what happened in San Diego, where the Cubs lost three straight games and a chance to reach their first World Series since 1945.

"Kind of reminds you of the Titanic," he said. "Only an act of God could keep them from the World Series. But I've gotten to know some of their players. They didn't want to be reminded of 1969 last year, and next year they won't want to be

Blackhawks great Bobby Hull (left) joins Ernie Banks and former Bears star Otis Wilson (right) at a tribute to the late broadcaster Harry Caray in March of 2012. (Phil Velasquez, Chicago Tribune)

reminded of 1984. I never looked back on 1969. If it wasn't meant to be, it wasn't meant to be."

Banks can't quite remember his best contract, but he thinks it was $65,000 in 1960 after he won back-to-back MVP awards. Third-base coaches make that now, but, naturally, Mr. Cub wishes everybody well.

"That's economics," he said. "Maybe I could have made more if I played somewhere else, but if they'd have traded me from Chicago, I'd have retired. There's more pressure with the money, too. Now it's must-win. When Mr. Wrigley ran the club, we wanted to win, but it was fun even if we didn't.

"It's more business now, which is understandable. That's why they're building bigger ballparks, that's why they're talking lights for Wrigley Field. I don't know what that would do with the mystique of the Cubs. I hate to see it, but that's progress. What time are we on the tee?"

Mr. Cub thwacks one last practice ball, and gathers his confidence.

"Good thing about golf is that you can make up for what you didn't get in baseball," Banks said. "Don Drysdale gave me trouble with the Dodgers, but I beat him in golf. Sandy Koufax, best pitcher I ever faced, I want to beat him next. The Dodgers were always tough on us, but I'm not finished with them. Go Cubbies." ▪

Ernie Banks, left, hands Sammy Sosa some fake currency in exchange for an autograph in March of 1999. Ernie asked Sammy to sign a baseball, and Sammy playfully said it would cost $45, which Ernie paid with bogus bills. (Phil Velasquez, Chicago Tribune)

Playing game of life – and winning

Originally published August 13, 2013

By David Haugh

Bizarre only to those who don't know Ernie Banks, Mr. Cub answered a question Monday asking what he did to deserve the Presidential Medal of Freedom by breaking into the song his buddy Sammy Davis Jr. made famous.

"Whether I'm right or whether I'm wrong. Whether I find a place in this world or never belong," Banks sang. "I gotta be me, I've gotta be me. What else can I be but what I am?"

What Banks was as a Hall of Famer who hit 512 home runs for the Cubs from 1953-71 opened his world to presidents and popes and allowed him to discuss poverty with Nelson Mandela and politics with Desmond Tutu. Banks' diverse collection of friends ranges from bleacher bums to billionaires like Warren Buffett, and the next stranger the nicest man in sports meets will be the first. As Chicago's foremost baseball ambassador, Banks slowly evolved into America's envoy for joy, someone whose indefatigable enthusiasm broke down social and racial barriers wherever he went.

And when the 82-year-old received the phone call recently confirming he would receive the country's highest civilian honor in November, Banks' mind went back to when he was a poor kid in Dallas and his dad bought his first baseball glove for $2.98.

"I look at my life and any of my 11 brothers or sisters could have done this too, so why me?" Banks told the Tribune. "When (presidential adviser) Valerie Jarrett called me, I said, 'Wow, are you kidding? The same award as (Negro Leagues legend) Buck O'Neil?' I've got to settle into the idea that Ernie, this is it. This is the pinnacle of what you've accomplished for the way you've led your life."

Has any athlete in Chicago led one more fascinating?

Banks won two most valuable player awards and made 11 All-Star teams as the best Cubs player ever but never made a secret that his biggest goal remained winning the Nobel Peace

In honor of his indomitable spirit, the statue of Ernie Banks outside Wrigley Field carries the inscription "Let's Play Two." (Phil Velasquez, Chicago Tribune)

"LET'S PLAY TWO"

Prize. Told Monday that this development might mean his legacy won't include a trip to Stockholm, Banks scoffed.

"I said I haven't done that ... yet," he cracked.

The quick wit and colorful banter Banks has become known for — "I'm 82 and know what to do," he rhymed — contrasts sharply with the youngster who heeded Dodgers legend Jackie Robinson's advice in 1954. Robinson, baseball's first African-American player in 1947, approached Banks, who became the Cubs' first black player six years later, before a game at Wrigley Field.

"Jackie came to our locker room on the third-base side and said, 'Ernie, I'm glad to see you're up here so now just listen and learn,'" Banks said. "For years, I didn't talk and learned a lot about people."

As Banks gradually felt the urge to be more vocal, he floated the idea past teammate Billy Williams. Williams and Banks routinely rode to work together via Lake Shore Drive.

"Billy would say, 'Ernie you see that lake? It's full of fish. When those fish open their mouths, they get caught. You see what I'm saying?'" Banks said. "I kept my mouth shut but tried to make a difference. My whole life, I've just wanted to make people better."

Whether it was an out-of-work fan looking for encouragement or a young player trying to make a mark in the majors, Banks sent the same message rooted in his own experiences: Believing leads to achieving; confidence grows from calm. A

Ernie Banks waves to fans at Wrigley Field on Tuesday, Aug.13, 2013, after being recognized for receiving the Presidential Medal of Freedom. (Nuccio DiNuzzo, Chicago Tribune)

favorite example involving ex-Cub and Cardinals great Lou Brock reinforced that.

"Lou was my roommate and so hard on himself he couldn't sleep, so one day (in 1962) he asked, 'Ernie, what does it take? I don't want to go back to Louisiana and chop no cotton,'" Banks said. "I finally told him: Learn to relax. The next game, he hit one of the longest home runs ever at the Polo Grounds. I asked, 'What happened?' He smiled and said, 'I relaxed.' So maybe I did do some good for people."

President Obama thinks so, and the irony of the White Sox's First Fan feting the Cubs' all-time most recognizable face isn't lost on Banks.

"I respect his White Sox loyalty because I've tried many times to get him to throw out the first pitch at Wrigley Field," Banks kidded.

That's where Banks will be honored Tuesday in a pregame ceremony surrounded by friends, including Williams and Reds manager Dusty Baker, and team officials past and present because, he contends, "without the Cubs, the fans or my teammates, none of this is possible."

The only thing more perfect for Banks would be a scheduled doubleheader so the Cubs could play two as tribute to the distinguished gentleman ultimately recognized for living every day like opening day. ▪

Right: Ernie Banks poses in front of his newly erected statue at Wrigley Field before the 2008 season opener. Opposite: Ernie Banks waves his cap to the Wrigley Field fans after throwing the ceremonial first pitch before a 2003 playoff game between the Cubs and the Braves. (Phil Velasquez, Chicago Tribune)

If racial bias hurt, he never showed it

Originally published January 25, 2015

By Fred Mitchell

Ernie Banks didn't call me back last week. I left voice messages, emailed him, sent him a text. That certainly wasn't like Ernie. He missed last weekend's Cubs Convention, and I wanted to do a well-being check on my longtime friend. He always would call me right back.

Then came the somber word on Jan. 23, 2015, that Mr. Cub had passed, just more than a week shy of his 84th birthday.

I was crushed, didn't get much sleep that night.

A flood of memories surfaced throughout the night as I repeated in my mind: "Remember the time when Ernie...?"

There are few opportunities in our profession to watch a superstar from our youth, then get to know him on a personal level well beyond his playing days. My friendship with Ernie began in the early '80s when I was the Cubs beat writer for the Tribune and he was working in various capacities for the ballclub.

I would call Ernie a pioneer for being the first African-American ballplayer for the Cubs. He would call me a pioneer for being the first African-American sportswriter for the Tribune.

During Black History Month a couple of years ago, the Cubs invited Banks and me to speak to a group of high school students about our respective career paths.

I joked that 1959 was a great year for both of us. Ernie won his second straight National League MVP award, and I was named MVP of West Gary Little League.

An avid golfer, Banks spoke of his friendship with Earl Woods, the late father of Tiger Woods. Earl Woods had been a catcher at Kansas State and the first African-American baseball player in the Big Eight Conference. Woods had turned down an offer to play for the Kansas City Monarchs of the Negro leagues to go to college. Banks played for the Monarchs before the Cubs signed him.

While we shared our individual stories with

Ernie Banks presents a trophy to Gary Wagner, 12, in July of 1964. Wagner was recognized as an outstanding student at the Ernie Banks Baseball School. (Chicago Tribune)

the youngsters, my role clearly was to moderate the discussion and steer Banks in the direction of defining his place in American society with regard to race relations.

Banks was en route to a Hall of Fame career by the late '50s. Yet there were restaurants in America where he was turned away, establishments he could not frequent and houses he could not rent or purchase because of the color of his skin.

Banks' fellow Hall of Fame teammate Billy Williams once told me in a book I co-authored with him that there were places in Mesa, Ariz., in the early '60s (where the Cubs still conduct spring training) that would not allow black Cubs players such as Banks, Lou Brock, Andre Rodgers, George Altman and Williams to rent.

"We don't mind, but our clients mind," was the most frequent response, Williams said.

Instead, the black players stayed in a shabby hotel in Phoenix they referred to as "the hut."

In 1961, when the Cubs would visit Houston — whose team was then known as the Colt 45s — the team's traveling secretary told Banks and other black players they were not allowed to venture downstairs to the hotel restaurant, Williams recalled. They were not welcome.

Yet more than 50 years later, Banks never expressed bitterness or resentment.

"He was always an individual who was the happy type," Ferguson Jenkins said Saturday night from Dallas. "He was always an optimist. You only saw the cheerful side of Ernie."

If he was hurting inside, Banks never showed it.

Ernie Banks, who served on the CTA's board of directors, shakes hands with conductor E.J. Roland while riding a train to Wrigley Field in June of 1970. (Arthur Walker, Chicago Tribune)

"I came from a segregated society, playing in the Negro leagues," Banks once told me. "Then I went into the military in the (recently desegregated) Army. So it was a learning experience for me to be with white players ... to play with them and go to lunch and dinner with them and ride on the planes with them. It was a learning experience.

"It was really different for me and (former Cubs second baseman) Gene Baker, who was a black player from Iowa. We just had to learn how to get along with people and keep our mouths shut."

Banks shares a Jan. 31 birthday with Major League Baseball trailblazer Jackie Robinson. They also shared a vision.

"Jackie Robinson, (on my first day) at Wrigley Field ... we played the Dodgers, and they had already (clinched) the pennant in September," Banks told me. "Jackie came over to me over at third base and said: 'We're glad to have you here, and I knew you would make it. ... But I would like to give you some advice: Just keep your mouth shut and you will learn.'

"And that's what I did for five years. I didn't talk very much. I just listened and I watched things and heard things. And I learned a lot from the segregated society to the integrated society."

Banks' ability to get along with people of all backgrounds did not go unnoticed.

"He was one of the great crossover baseball players of his day as he made the transition from the Negro Baseball leagues to Major League Baseball," Rev. Jesse Jackson of the Rainbow PUSH Coalition

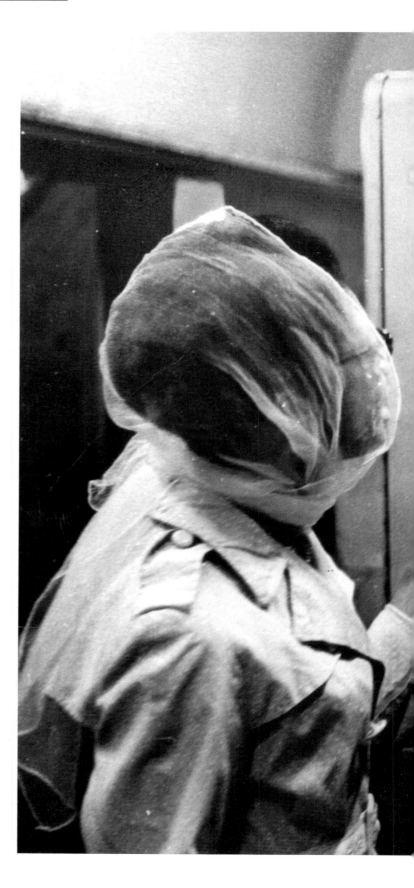

Always approachable, Ernie Banks chats with a fan at a CTA subway station while waiting for the train to Wrigley Field in June of 1970. (Arthur Walker, Chicago Tribune)

said in a statement. "He was not only a great baseball player, but beyond his talent as a shortstop and eventually a first baseman, was his character, his eternal optimism — 'let's play two today' — and his personality was a racial bridge builder."

One of Banks' unfinished projects was an attempt to reconcile the estrangement between the Cubs and Sammy Sosa.

Banks visited Sosa over the years and played golf with him in the Dominican Republic. I interviewed Sosa in the Dominican during that same time period in an attempt to have him come clean about alleged steroid abuse.

"He can admit to that," Banks said when Sosa was not invited to the Cubs 100-year Wrigley Field celebration. "We had Barry Bonds, Mark McGwire ... a lot of guys ... Alex Rodriguez. They admitted to doing something that is not right. But I don't know if Sammy ever admitted to that.

"(Sosa) did a lot for this organization. And nobody could answer (why he was not at the celebration). I wanted him to come. And later on it came out that Sammy wanted to come. Nobody invited him."

Banks' message for everyone was pretty basic and clear: Treat people the way you want to be treated and be forgiving. Listen to those who are more experienced. And don't be afraid to dream big.

I was not able to reach Ernie on the phone last week. But here he is now, still speaking to me. ■

Shown here in California in 2005, Ernie Banks was known for his positive attitude and unfailing optimism. (Phil Velasquez, Chicago Tribune)

With (from left) Fergie Jenkins, Rev Jesse Jackson, Hank Aaron and Billy Williams behind him, Ernie Banks tosses a ball during ceremonies before the Cubs' 2008 opener at Wrigley Field. (Phil Velasquez, Chicago Tribune)

Behind the sunny disposition, a competitive fire burned

Originally published January 30, 1996

By Jerome Holtzman

Ernie Banks is not the type to spend much time on regrets or envy — except for a fleeting moment during the 1977 World Series when Reggie Jackson crashed three home runs on three consecutive pitches, all off different pitchers.

"I used to dream about playing in the World Series," Banks said on the eve of his 65th birthday in 1996. "It was always the seventh game. When Reggie Jackson hit those three home runs, it was me doing that."

When Banks would see Jackson at banquets and at celebrity golf tournaments, he'd share that dream with the former A's and Yankees slugger. "I tell him, 'Reggie, that was me.'"

But it wasn't. Reggie was Mr. October. Banks holds the all-time record of most games played — 2,528 from 1953-71, all 19 seasons with the Cubs — without appearing in a single playoff or World Series game.

"I'd rather be Mr. Cub," Banks said.

He hung it up after the 1971 season, two years before the inception of the designated hitter.

"I would have liked to be a DH," Banks said.

"I'll tell you something I've never told anybody before. In '69, when I was 38, I thought about playing only home games, not going on the road. A couple of times I started out to see (team owner) Mr. (Phil) Wrigley. But I always got cold feet. It would have created too much tension for him. There couldn't be one rule for me, and another rule for the other 24 players."

There should have been.

Without question, Banks was the best and most productive hitter in Chicago baseball history: 512 career home runs; five seasons, including four in a row, 40 or more home runs; six seasons, 100 or more runs batted in; winner of the National League's Most Valuable Player award two years in succession, the first player honored twice from

Still sunny at age 74, Ernie Banks is photographed at the Ritz-Carlton Marina Del Rey in California on July 19, 2005. (Phil Velasquez, Chicago Tribune)

a second-division club; five grand slam home runs in one season, a record since broken by the Yankees' Don Mattingly.

Most fans may not be aware but Banks also set the one-season fielding record for shortstops: fewest errors, 12, and highest fielding percentage, 875. He was also an iron man. He has the record for most consecutive games from the start of a major-league career, 424, and later, a streak of 717 games, longest for an active player at that time.

Banks seldom complained. So far as I can recall, the only time I saw him upset was when Sandy Grady, a Philadelphia sports columnist, described him as having "pencil-thin" shoulders. For days Banks walked around saying "pencil-thin shoulders," sometimes with a smile, sometimes not.

It peeved him because there were many references to his slender build. Meeting him for the first time many people were surprised he wasn't bigger, with bulging muscles. But his power was generated by his hips and legs.

Probably because he was on an optimist beyond compare, always predicting a Cub pennant, often in verse, he seldom was acknowledged as a tough competitor. But behind his cheerful manner lurked a ferocious desire.

Banks hit three home runs in a game four times. In 1962, Moe Drabowsky, a former teammate then with Milwaukee, hit him on the

In a pre-game ceremony recognizing his Presidential Medal of Freedom, Ernie Banks hugs former teammate Billy Williams on Aug. 13, 2013 at Wrigley Field. (Nuccio DiNuzzo, Chicago Tribune)

"In '69, when I was 38, I thought about playing only home games, not going on the road." –Ernie Banks

back of the head. For the first time, Banks decided it was time for him to wear a batting helmet. When he returned four days later, he hit three home runs and a double.

He was also a favorite target of Don Newcombe, the Dodgers' hard-throwing right-hander.

"He used to hit Gene Baker and me," Banks recalled. "Campy (Roy Campanella, Newcombe's catcher) would sit behind the plate and warn us. He would say, 'Watch out, the next one's coming at your head!'"

During 1958, after he either was hit or knocked down by Bob Purkey, Don Drysdale, Jack Sanford and Bob Friend, he hit the next pitch for a home run.

"I didn't think anybody remembered that," Banks said, pleased with the recollection. "Alvin Dark (then a teammate) talked about it a lot. He'd say, 'Knock Ernie down and he'll kill you.'" ■

Ernie Banks looks up at his statue after it was unveiled outside Wrigley Field on March 31, 2008. (Charles Cherney, Chicago Tribune)

Always sunny

Originally published January 24, 2015

By Paul Sullivan

Ernie Banks didn't invent day baseball or help build Wrigley Field.

He just made the idea of playing a baseball game under the sun at the corner of Clark and Addison streets sound like a day in paradise, win or lose.

That optimistic attitude, from a man who never experienced the limelight of a World Series — or a postseason, for that matter — is what made the Hall of Famer "Mr. Cub," and one of the most iconic athletes in Chicago history. His death Friday at 83 was a shock to most of us, even though he missed the Cubs Convention last weekend, a party he had loved attending over the years.

Ernie was so full of life, it seemed like he would live forever, shouting, "Let's play two!" and perennially making up a song on the spot informing us that this year is the one we've been waiting for all of our lives. And if it wasn't? There was always next year.

He was a player who promoted the game like he was part of the marketing department. Not because he had to, but because he truly loved the Cubs and the game itself.

I was fortunate enough to get to know Banks from covering the Cubs, and he was always gracious and fun-loving, whether at the park or in spring training. The last time I got to talk to him was last summer before Greg Maddux's Hall of Fame induction in Cooperstown, N.Y., where Banks showed up at the party to fete his fellow Cubs legend.

I was amazed at how energetic and enthusiastic Banks appeared, even though he obviously was getting on in years and moving a bit more slowly. On the plane trip back to Chicago, a problem with the jetway forced the plane to sit on the tarmac at O'Hare for 30 minutes while we waited for someone to come and fix it.

Banks stood near the door the whole time, patiently waiting, smiling and interacting with fans. He had no time for misplaced anger at something he had no control over. Every day was a beautiful day for Mr. Cub, and nothing was

With fellow Hall-of-Fame shortstops Robin Yount on his left and Cal Ripken on his right, Ernie Banks salutes the crowd at the 2008 All-Star Game at Yankee Stadium. (Phil Velasquez, Chicago Tribune)

going to spoil his mood.

It may not have been that way his entire life, but it certainly became his persona as a Cub. Banks told Sports Illustrated in the summer he had difficulty at first dealing with Cubs manager Leo Durocher, an ornery type who gave him a hard time because he could.

"I went to my mother with that one," he said. "She said, 'Ernie, kill 'em with kindness.' And that's what I did."

That kindness was obvious everywhere Banks went. His mentor was former Negro leaguer Buck O'Neil, who had a similar personality and love for the game.

Ernie was always in the mood for talking, and he treated everyone like he had known them his entire life. You would sometimes wonder how anyone could be so "up" all the time, whether he was just doing it because that's what everyone expected from him.

But after a while you realized it was just Ernie being Ernie.

Most great players are remembered for their stats or their style of play.

Banks always will be remembered for showing us how to enjoy life every single day.

No one enjoyed it more than Ernie Banks, and Wrigley Field never will be the same without him. ■

Right: Ernie Banks waves to the crowd at the 2014 Cubs convention. (Phil Velasquez, Chicago Tribune) Opposite: Ernie Banks dances with Cubs owner Laura Ricketts during a ceremony honoring him for receiving the Presidential Medal of Freedom on Aug.13, 2013. (Nuccio DiNuzzo, Chicago Tribune)

So long, Mr. Cub

Originally published February 1, 2015

By Paul Sullivan

Of all the talents Ernie Banks exhibited over his Hall of Fame career, perhaps the most impressive was his ability to relate to everyday people from all walks of life.

"He could make you feel like you were the most important person in the universe," longtime friend John Rogers said during Banks' memorial service at Fourth Presbyterian Church.

That was the thematic motif as family, friends and fans congregated to celebrate the life of the legendary ballplayer, who died Jan. 23 at 83.

Almost every speaker drove the point home that Banks was not just a great athlete who loved the game. He was simply a man who enjoyed meeting and talking to people, leaving a little piece of himself with hundreds and hundreds of those fortunate enough to run into him, whether it was at the ballpark, walking down the street or in the aisle of a grocery store.

"Ernie walked up to you as if he had known you for years," Billy Williams said.

"He branded goodwill," Rev. Jesse Jackson added.

It's a lesson that should be taught to every athlete, especially the ones who feel smothered by the fame that comes with the territory. How many times have I seen ballplayers whip out their cellphones and pretend to make a call as they leave a ballpark, giving them cover from fans who may want an autograph or just a chance to say hello?

Perhaps there are some fans whom Banks ignored. He was human, after all. But judging from the emails and conversations I've had with those who randomly bumped into him over the years, those stories are few and far between. He genuinely liked people.

"Ernie Banks is not Mr. Cub because we loved him," Cubs Chairman Tom Ricketts said. "Ernie Banks is Mr. Cub because he loved us back. As it turned out, Ernie became Mr. Cub through no more magic than just being himself."

Banks' memorial was as comforting as a soft summer breeze, with former teammate Williams stealing the show with stories of their conversations about life as roommates or sharing rides to work.

Banks once told notorious knockdown pitcher Bob Gibson that Williams was going to hit a home run off him that day, prompting Williams to plead with his friend, "Ernie, don't make him meaner, man."

Ernie Banks' funeral procession passes by the Friendly Confines of Wrigley Field. (Abel Uribe, Chicago Tribune)

> "Ernie Banks is not Mr. Cub because we loved him. Banks is Mr. Cub because he loved us back. As it turned out, Ernie became Mr. Cub through no more magic than just being himself." –Tom Ricketts

Banks' son, Joey, thanked his father for "showing us how to be winners without winning all the time." Joey's twin brother, Jerry, revealed one of Ernie's favorite sayings: "I feel like I could fly."

After the service, Cubs broadcaster Pat Hughes told a story on the church steps of how Banks was at a big party and told all the kids, "The best thing you can do when you get back to the hotel, rub your daddy's feet."

"My daughters come back giggling to me, 'Daddy, Ernie Banks said we should rub your feet,'" Hughes said. "Everyone in the whole room is laughing about Ernie. He brought everyone together. It was a funny, off-the-wall, quirky thing to do, but it spread joy, and that's what Ernie loved to do."

That's why Banks had such an impact on the city and why his death was felt by so many who didn't even know him. Cubs fan Tom Moroz, of Uptown, was one of several hundred waiting near Wrigley Field to get a glimpse of the procession as it drove past.

"I was watching on TV and shedding tears when they were wheeling his casket out of the church," Moroz said. "I thought I have to come down to the ballpark. (The procession) passed quickly. I thought they may stop, but that didn't happen. But you could clearly see the No. 14 (flag) draped over the casket in the back."

The ballpark construction continued after the procession disappeared up Clark Street, and fans went back into the nearby bars and restaurants, or just went home.

Before you know it, opening day will arrive, and the Cubs' attempt to end their title drought will begin anew.

It won't be the same, of course, but rest assured the spirit of Ernie Banks will always remain a part of Wrigley Field, come rain or shine. ∎

Ernie Banks' granddaughter Courtney Dozier Banks touches the casket before the funeral service. (John J. Kim, Chicago Tribune)

Ernie by the numbers

Banks' career statistics and Cubs' year-by-year record

YEAR	G	AB	R	H	2B	3B	HR	RBI	AVG	OBP	SLG	W	L	T	PCT	FINISH (GB)
1953	10	35	3	11	1	1	2	6	.314	.385	.571	65	89	1	.422	7th of 8 (40)
1954	154	593	70	163	19	7	19	79	.275	.326	.427	64	90	0	.416	7th of 8 (33)
1955	154	596	98	176	29	9	44	117	.295	.345	.596	72	81	1	.441	6th of 8 (26)
1956	139	538	82	160	25	8	28	85	.297	.358	.530	60	94	3	.390	8th of 8 (33)
1957	156	594	113	169	34	6	43	102	.285	.360	.579	62	92	2	.403	7th of 8 (33)
1958	154	617	119	193	23	11	47	129	.313	.366	.614	72	82	0	.468	5th of 8 (20)
1959	155	589	97	179	25	6	45	143	.304	.374	.596	74	80	1	.481	5th of 8 (13)
1960	156	597	94	162	32	7	41	117	.271	.350	.554	60	94	2	.390	7th of 8 (35)
1961	138	511	75	142	22	4	29	80	.278	.346	.507	64	90	2	.416	7th of 8 (29)
1962	154	610	87	164	20	6	37	104	.269	.306	.503	59	103	0	.364	9th of 10 (42.5)
1963	130	432	41	98	20	1	18	64	.227	.292	.403	82	80	0	.506	7th of 10 (17)
1964	157	591	67	156	29	6	23	95	.264	.307	.450	76	86	0	.469	8th of 10 (17)
1965	163	612	79	162	25	3	28	106	.265	.328	.453	72	90	2	.444	8th of 10 (25)
1966	141	511	52	139	23	7	15	75	.272	.315	.432	59	103	0	.364	10th of 10 (36)
1967	151	573	68	158	26	4	23	95	.276	.31	.455	87	74	1	.540	3rd of 10 (14)
1968	150	552	71	136	27	0	32	83	.246	.287	.469	84	78	1	.519	3rd of 10 (13)
1969	155	565	60	143	19	2	23	106	.253	.309	.416	92	70	1	.568	2nd of 6 (8)
1970	72	222	25	56	6	2	12	44	.252	.313	.459	84	78	0	.519	2nd of 6 (5)
1971	39	83	4	16	2	0	3	6	.193	.247	.325	83	79	0	.512	3rd of 6 (14)
Totals	2528	9421	1305	2583	407	90	512	1636	.274	.330	.500	1,371	1,633	17	.456	

Where Banks ranks

Category	Number	Cubs rank*	MLB rank*
Games played	2,528	1st	48th
Hits	2,583	2nd	86th
Extra-base hits	1,009	1st	35th
Home runs	512	2nd	22nd (tied)
Runs batted in	1,636	2nd	29th
Total bases	4,706	1st	34th

* Rank through end of 2014 season.

Long since retired but still beloved, Ernie Banks acknowledges the Wrigley Fans before the playoff opener against the Padres on Oct. 2, 1984. (Ed Wagner, Jr., Chicago Tribune)

Wearing an Ernie Banks jersey, Dick Martin of Grayslake salutes the late Cub's casket at the public visitation. "He was my idol," Martin said. "He was my hero." (John J. Kim, Chicago Tribune)